WORKBOOK 4

prepared for the course team by bob kelly

This publication forms part of an Open University course DD100 *An Introduction to the Social Sciences: Understanding Social Change.* Details of this and other Open University courses can be obtained from the Call Centre, PO Box 724, The Open University, Milton Keynes MK7 6ZS, United Kingdom: tel. +44 (0)1908 653231, e-mail ces-gen@open.ac.uk

Alternatively, you may visit the Open University website at http://www.open.ac.uk where you can learn more about the wide range of courses and packs offered at all levels by The Open University.

To purchase this publication or other components of Open University courses, contact Open University Worldwide Ltd, The Berrill Building, Walton Hall, Milton Keynes MK7 6AA, United Kingdom: tel. +44 (0)1908 858785; fax +44 (0)1908 858787; e-mail ouwenq@open.ac.uk; website http://www.ouw.co.uk

The Open University
Walton Hall, Milton Keynes
MK7 6AA

First published 2000. Second edition 2001

Edited, designed and typeset by The Open University.

Printed in the United Kingdom by The Bath Press, Bath.

ISBN 0 7492 7733 5

2.1

19894B/dd100wb4isbn0749277335i2.1

Contents

The DD100 course team

John Allen, *Senior Lecturer in Geography*

Penny Bennett, *Editor*

Pam Berry, *Compositor*

Simon Bromley, *Senior Lecturer in Government*

David Calderwood, *Project Controller*

Elizabeth Chaplin, *Tutor Panel*

Giles Clark, *Co-publishing Advisor*

Stephen Clift, *Editor*

Allan Cochrane, *Professor of Public Policy*

Lene Connolly, *Print Buying Controller*

Graham Dawson, *Lecturer in Economics*

Lesley Duguid, *Senior Course Co-ordination Secretary*

Fran Ford, *Senior Course Co-ordination Secretary*

David Goldblatt, *Co-Course Team Chair, Lecturer in Government*

Jenny Gove, *Lecturer in Psychology*

Judith Greene, *Professor of Psychology*

Montserrat Guibernau, *Lecturer in Government*

Peter Hamilton, *Lecturer in Sociology*

Celia Hart, *Picture Researcher*

David Held, *Professor of Politics and Sociology*

Susan Himmelweit, *Senior Lecturer in Economics*

Steve Hinchliffe, *Lecturer in Geography*

Anne Howells, *Project Controller*

Gordon Hughes, *Lecturer in Social Policy*

Christina Janoszka, *Course Manager*

Pat Jess, *Staff Tutor in Geography (Region 12)*

Bob Kelly, *Staff Tutor in Government (Region 06)*

Margaret Kiloh, *Staff Tutor in Applied Social Sciences (Region 13)*

Sylvia Lay-Flurrie, *Secretary*

Siân Lewis, *Graphic Designer*

Tony McGrew, *Professor of International Relations, University of Southampton*

Hugh Mackay, *Staff Tutor in Sociology (Region 10)*

Maureen Mackintosh, *Professor of Economics*

Eugene McLaughlin, *Senior Lecturer in Applied Social Science*

Andrew Metcalf, *Senior Producer, BBC*

Gerry Mooney, *Staff Tutor in Applied Social Sciences (Region 11)*

Ray Munns, *Graphic Artist*

Kathy Pain, *Staff Tutor in Geography (Region 02)*

Clive Pearson, *Tutor Panel*

Lynne Poole, *Tutor Panel*

Norma Sherratt, *Staff Tutor in Sociology (Region 03)*

Roberto Simonetti, *Lecturer in Economics*

Dick Skellington, *Project Officer*

Brenda Smith, *Staff Tutor in Psychology (Region 12)*

Mark Smith, *Lecturer in Social Sciences*

Grahame Thompson, *Professor of Political Economy*

Ken Thompson, *Professor of Sociology*

Stuart Watt, *Lecturer in Psychology/KMI*

Andy Whitehead, *Graphic Artist*

Kath Woodward, *Co-Course Team Chair, Staff Tutor in Sociology (Region 07)*

Chris Wooldridge, *Editor*

External Assessor

Nigel Thrift, *Professor of Geography, University of Bristol*

INTRODUCTION

Welcome to Block 4 of the course, on which you will be working for the next five weeks. The workbook will again be your guide through your studies. Before you begin work on Book 4 and the other course materials there are several important matters that we need to bring to your attention.

Block overview

As with the earlier blocks of study, Block 4 combines a range of teaching materials, the textbook *A Globalizing World? Culture, Economics, Politics*, two audio-cassettes, a study skills supplement on reading maps, a TV programme, and this workbook. The recommended study timetable and path through this are shown in Figures 1 and 2.

Study week	Course material	Suggested study time
21	*Workbook 4* and Book 4: *A Globalizing World? Culture, Economics, Politics* Introduction Chapter 1 Audio-cassette 7, Side A and notes	11 hours 1 hour
22	Workbook and Chapter 2 Audio-cassette 7, Side B and notes	11 hours 1 hour
23	Workbook and Chapter 3 Audio-cassette 8, Side A and notes	10 hours 2 hours
24	Workbook, Chapter 4 and Afterword *Study Skills Supplement 3: Reading Maps* plus Audio-cassette 8, Side B TV 04 and notes	10 hours 1 hour 1 hour
25	TMA 04	12 hours

FIGURE 1   Course materials for Block 4

FIGURE 2 Recommended study route for Block 4

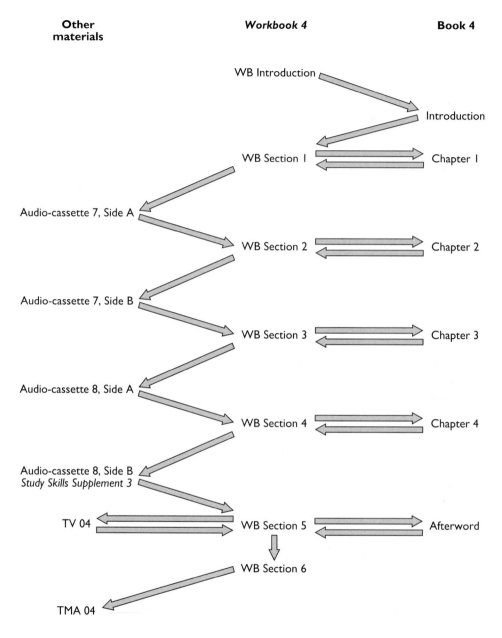

Block 4 presents a shift in direction on DD100, both in terms of the key questions which focus on the global arena and the UK's place in the world, and in our development of the circuit of knowledge, to focus on different *theories* of how knowledge is produced. You have met different claims which use evidence to support particular theoretical positions before in DD100. In Block 4 we take the focus on theories further and work on developing the **very important skills** which will enable you to evaluate different theories in the social sciences by means of the tests of *coherence, empirical adequacy* and *comprehensiveness*.

Key questions

In this block the focus of attention switches. Most of the course, so far, has studied the UK state, economy and society. Block 4 looks at the global and the United Kingdom's place in the world. It asks what impact changing information systems and patterns of world trade have on individual states such as the UK, and whether these states and societies can still determine their own policies and priorities. We have broken down these issues into four key questions that run throughout Block 4.

I   What is globalization?

A range of evidence suggests that events in other parts of the world continually affect our lives; for example: problems of environmental pollution, the activities of foreign-owned corporations, or wars between and within other states. But how should we best describe or conceptualize globalization? What areas of social life does it apply to?

2   How significant is contemporary globalization?

A quick glance at the historical record suggests that long-distance and socially-significant interactions between societies are hardly new. Islam, in the space of a few centuries, had spread from its Arabian heartland to Spain in the West and northern India in the East, transforming religious, cultural and political life in every society along the way. Moreover, complex and intense long-distance relationships of trade, pilgrimage and military alliance across the Islamic lands meant that a high level of interaction was maintained. Closer to the present, the late nineteenth century saw an enormous expansion of global military, economic and political interconnections as European empires stretched to every continent. So is there anything distinctively new about contemporary forms of globalization? Is it the sheer quantity and speed of global interactions that differentiates the present from the past? Is the geography of interaction different?

3   What is the impact of globalization on the sovereignty and autonomy of nation-states?

Look at a map of the world today and it is almost entirely carved up into separate, bordered nation-states. As you will know from your work on nations and nationalism in Block 1, within each of those territorially demarcated areas, the state claims to be *sovereign*; that it above all possesses exclusive and rightful jurisdiction as the highest legal authority in the land. Moreover, sovereign states claim to be able to shape practically the destinies of their citizens, independently of outside forces, and thus possess *autonomy*. But in a world where states have signed up to all kinds of global legal documents, human rights charters and international organizations, what is left of their individual sovereignty? More to the point, in a world where drugs and money cross borders with impunity, can a single nation-state really solve its own drug problems or regulate its economy by itself? If governments can't automatically control these things, can anyone or any organization? If someone or a body has such control, is there any democratic accountability?

4   Are there winners and losers in globalization?

How are the costs and benefits of social change triggered by globalization distributed? Does the global economy, for example, enrich some at the expense of others? Within the UK, are some classes and regions benefiting from free trade and global financial deregulation and others suffering? Across the world, how do these 'goods' and 'bads' get distributed? Are there some social groups or whole societies who are not even part of global networks?

Alongside these four questions, we will also be asking you to think through and try to reframe these issues in terms of the course themes. One way of thinking this through for *uncertainty and diversity* and *structure and agency* would be:

- To what extent does globalization create a more uncertain environment for individual societies and states?

- Does global interconnectedness and access to the global flow of ideas and cultures encourage greater diversity within societies? Can it lead to a greater resistance to outside influences? Does it lead to the creation of a bland and uniform global culture?

- To what extent do global structures – supranational institutions, global flows of information, patterns of global trade and investment – shape and constrain the agency of individuals, firms and governments? What opportunities does globalization create?

The role of changing flows and forms of knowledge and information is also a feature of this block. We want you to focus on the analytical strand of *knowledge and knowing* in this block and to do so as part of the key skills work.

Key skills

Evaluating social science claims and theories

In earlier chapters of this course you have met a range of theories which attempt to explain a whole variety of types of individual behaviour and patterns of social change: the causes of crime, the origins of nationalism, the creation of human intelligence, etc.

Moreover, you will have often found that we have presented more than one theoretical explanation of crime or nationalism. The questions will have certainly occurred to you, which theory is stronger?, or more valuable?, or more accurate? Answering these questions draws on the process of *evaluation*; it is the key skill that this block works on and forms the final element of the circuit of knowledge (Figure 3).

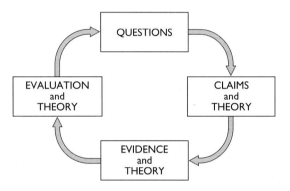

FIGURE 3   The circuit of knowledge

Evaluating *claims* and *theories* in the social sciences is a complex and much contested terrain; in DD100 we have chosen to use three *tests* as our tools of evaluation. Simply put, those tests are:

●   Is the claim or theory *coherent*?

●   How well does the claim or theory account for *empirical evidence*?

●   How *comprehensive* an explanation does the claim or theory generate?

For shorthand purposes we will call these tests of evaluation: *coherence*, *empirical adequacy*, and *comprehensiveness*.

Coherence

In general there are three ways of testing the coherence of a claim or theory. First, we can look at the clarity of the key claims and concepts. Second, we can look at how logical the links are in the chain of reasoning that makes up the theory. Third, we can examine the plausibility and accuracy of the often unspoken or hidden assumptions that those concepts and chains of reasoning rest upon.

These rather abstract tests are best illustrated by looking at a simple theory or claim. For example, the liberal political tradition, which you encountered in Block 3, has always argued that *democracy is good for economic growth*.

How could we begin to test the coherence of this claim?

In terms of *conceptual clarity* we might ask what precisely is meant by the key terms. Democracy comes in many forms and many shades of grey, so what exactly are the criteria for saying whether a society is democratic or authoritarian? Do societies have to possess all the features of democracy, such as universal suffrage, to generate economic growth or just some, such as the rule of law? And what is meant by good here? – a sharper description of the causal relationship between democratic politics and economic growth is required.

This could take us to the *chain of reasoning*. To really explore this we would need to know a lot more about the details of the liberal argument than support the claim we have been looking at. One version of the chain of reasoning might look like this:

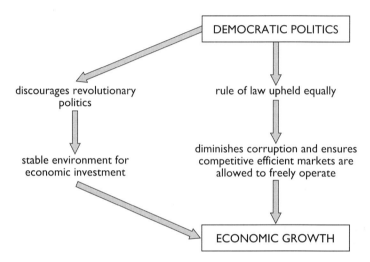

Pressing this further in terms of its *chain of reasoning* and *unspoken assumptions* we could ask:

- Why does democratic politics discourage revolutionary politics? Doesn't authoritarian politics do the same? Could we argue that oppression can also deter possible opposition?

- Is the rule of law the only or the main reason for diminishing corruption? Do organizational systems and practices prevent or deter corruption? Do particular cultures encourage or discourage corruption?

- A key assumption buried in this chain of reasoning concerns the relationship between free markets and growth. Are free markets the main source of economic growth? If so, why?

Empirical adequacy

As we have argued throughout DD100, gathering and organizing empirical evidence is only one step in the circuit of knowledge – you have to do something with it. That something is an essential element of the process of evaluation. Tests of *empirical adequacy* – how claims and theories fare when actually faced with information about the world – fall into a number of categories.

First, evidence may support or *verify* a theory. To continue with our example, if a theory claims that democracy is good for economic growth, then evidence of countries with democratic politics and high rates of economic growth would help verify the theory. However, evidence may also refute or *falsify* a theory.

What sort of evidence would falsify our theory about democracy and economic growth?

Examples would include authoritarian societies with high rates of economic growth (such as South Korea in the 1970s or China in the 1990s) or democratic societies with low rates of economic growth (such as the UK in the 1970s or Germany in the 1990s).

Comprehensiveness

The test of *comprehensiveness* can also be understood in a number of different ways. First we can ask how broad the coverage of a theory is in time and space. Does the liberal theory of the relationship between democracy and economic growth stand for all types of societies and all historical periods or just some? The rather awkward cases of authoritarian East Asian societies with high rates of growth could be explained away by restricting the comprehensiveness of the theory to European and North American societies. Even then it might be in trouble when looking at the case of pre-First World War Germany (rapid growth and limited democratic politics).

Another test of comprehensiveness would be how many facets of social life a theory incorporates. In the case of democracy and economic growth, the liberal theory is quite narrow. It does not take into account the possibilities that specifically economic or cultural structures, or even wider global conditions, might shape economic growth. Of course, a more elaborate, comprehensive account of economic growth has been constructed by liberals from the crude model presented here.

- The key skill developed in Block 4 is *evaluating* claims and theories.

- Evaluating is based on three tests: *coherence, empirical adequacy* and *comprehensiveness.*

- The test of coherence includes examining the clarity of concepts, the logic of the links between them, and the unspoken assumptions that underpin them.

- The test of empirical adequacy leads to verification or falsification of a theory.

- The test of comprehensiveness asks about the spatial and temporal scope of a theory and its internal complexity.

Having subjected theories to these tests, a question of comparison remains. We might find that one theory stands up well to empirical evidence but is hopelessly narrow and incomprehensive in its coverage. Should we prefer this to a theory that stands up to the evidence less well, but offered itself up to the possibility of falsification by being much more bold, complex and comprehensive in the type of argument it sought to make? What if, in both cases, the theories possessed clear flaws in the chain of reasoning or implausible assumptions about the world? Do they become useless? We will return to some of these issues in Section 5 of the workbook. However, what is certain is that a new set of unexpected *questions* will have been raised that require further investigation.

Assessing Block 4

The pattern for this block is the same as for Blocks 1 and 2 in that the fifth week of work is devoted to the production of an assignment (TMA 04) to send to your tutor. The assignment will take the form of a 1,500 word essay which will ask you to evaluate a theory or theories of globalization.

In Section 6 of this workbook we will set a 'mock' assignment that will be similar to the actual one you will face, and we will give you some guidance on how to tackle it. Our aim here is to give you a grounding in the skill of evaluation and to encourage you to think about it as you work your way through the course material.

 Now please read the Introduction to Book 4, *A Globalizing World?* Then return to this point in the workbook.

1 A GLOBALIZING SOCIETY?

So what is *globalization*? How significant is it? How does it affect our lives? How do social scientists interpret it and evaluate it? Each chapter of *A Globalizing World?* will focus on a particular dimension of globalization to illustrate these issues and debates, with authors consciously emphasizing different approaches to the topic.

In Chapter 1 we will be introducing you to three basic interpretations of global developments that we broadly classify as the views of *globalists*, *traditionalists* and *transformationalists*. The general characteristics of each of these approaches are laid out in Chapter 1, but it does need to be pointed out that we have simplified a vast array of complex material into three apparently distinct groupings. Each approach can be further sub-divided, and there is plenty of interweaving and overlap between the approaches. Our aim has not been to distort the arguments, but simply to present them in an accessible manner which enables you to engage in the important tasks of understanding, analysing and evaluating contrasting positions. If and when you go on to study further courses in the social sciences, the greater richness and complexity of these debates will be revealed.

Before we launch you into the actual debates, we want you to consider some of your own experiences and views on the relevant issues.

To begin with, let's accept for now the idea that the world is becoming a *smaller* place, that distances and the time taken to travel them have shrunk, and that what happens in your locality and the country in general is now greatly affected by what goes on in other parts of the globe.

WORKBOOK ACTIVITY 1.1

Just take a couple of minutes on this. Make a list of specific examples of the world 'becoming smaller' that you have experienced or read about which make life different now from, say, 20 or 30 years ago.

COMMENT

We won't give you our own specific answers to this as it is *your view* and experiences that matter. We can imagine a range of very different answers and examples that you may have come up with, *but we are confident that you will have found it quite easy to think of examples.*

It is important to consider cultural, economic and political dimensions of globalization and the possible relationships between them.

Try to identify the possible role of each of these dimensions in relation to these questions:

- Why do we now buy so much more imported food than in the past?

- Why are particular factories/businesses opening and closing?

- Why is there so much international news in the press and on television?

Do bear these questions in mind when you read the debates that follow – if 'globalization' really is occurring then it must have effects for all of us that are experienced in everyday situations, and it is important to understand both its causes and its effects.

The first chapter of Book 4 will introduce you to many of the key terms and theories that surround questions of globalization to set up debates that will reoccur in different forms throughout the book. It will also present you with indicators that offer ways of testing the accuracy and relevance of the competing theories, including quantitative and qualitative evidence.

KEY TASKS

Chapter 1, 'A Globalizing Society?'

- To understand the general concept of globalization.

- To be able to distinguish the theoretical approaches associated with *globalists, traditionalists* and *transformationalists*, and be able to compare and contrast them.

- To understand the range of evidence which can be drawn upon to evaluate competing theories.

Now please read Chapter I and then return here. As usual you should spend about two-thirds of your time on the chapter and around one-third on this section of the workbook.

1.1 Extracting the key points from Chapter I

If you have been following the advice given in earlier workbooks your approach to reading and understanding the chapter will have probably been:

- to skim read the chapter, taking particular note of headings, summaries, etc.;

- to remind yourself of points raised in the book Introduction and earlier parts of the workbook as to what the key questions and issues of the chapter will be; and

- to actively read the chapter, taking brief notes/highlighting points as appropriate in one or more of the ways that you feel most helpful.

If you have been able to do all this you may find that some of the activities that follow have already been completed to your satisfaction.

The key role of Chapter 1 was to open up the concept of *globalization* and the various interpretations and assessments of it.

WORKBOOK ACTIVITY 1.2

Skim your own notes on Chapter 1. How could you present them concisely to summarize the chapter at a glance?

C O M M E N T _____

Our notes looked like this.

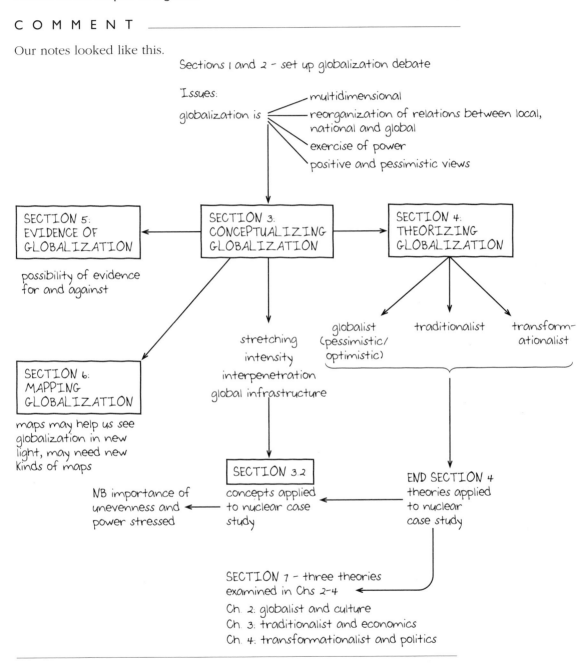

Sections 1 and 2 – set up globalization debate

Issues:
globalization is
— multidimensional
— reorganization of relations between local, national and global
— exercise of power
— positive and pessimistic views

SECTION 5:
EVIDENCE OF
GLOBALIZATION

possibility of evidence
for and against

SECTION 3:
CONCEPTUALIZING
GLOBALIZATION

SECTION 4:
THEORIZING
GLOBALIZATION

stretching
intensity
interpenetration
global infrastructure

globalist
(pessimistic/
optimistic)   traditionalist   transform-
                                              ationalist

SECTION 6:
MAPPING
GLOBALIZATION

maps may help us see
globalization in new
light, may need new
kinds of maps

NB importance of
unevenness and
power stressed

SECTION 3.2
concepts applied
to nuclear case
study

END SECTION 4
theories applied
to nuclear
case study

SECTION 7 – three theories
examined in Chs 2-4
Ch. 2: globalist and culture
Ch. 3: traditionalist and economics
Ch. 4: transformationalist and politics

If this is the basic skeleton of the chapter, how will you be able to use and develop the material here?

● In Section 1.2 of the workbook you will be looking at concepts of globalization and evidence for globalization.

- In Section 1.3 you will be looking in more detail at the theories of globalization.

- The material on mapping globalization will be returned to in connection with *Study Skills Supplement 3: Reading Maps* (which you will be studying in week 24).

In this section we want you to take another look at the material in Section 2.2 of Chapter 1 and reframe it in terms of two of the course themes. Then we will reflect on your understanding of some of the terms raised in the chapter.

WORKBOOK ACTIVITY 1.3

Look back at Readings 1.1 (Will Hutton), 1.2 (Geoff Mulgan) and 1.4 (Anthony Giddens) of Chapter 1. To what extent and in what way does the account of globalization in each extract:

- connect globalization to *uncertainty*?

- connect globalization to an increase or decrease in *diversity*?

- think about globalization in terms of *structure* and *agency*?

COMMENT

Reading 1.1: Will Hutton

Strongly suggests that globalization superficially increases diversity due to the diffusion of global brands. The English language diminishes diversity as everywhere becomes the same.

Reading 1.2: Geoff Mulgan

Mulgan notes differences between rich and poor in the face of globalization, suggesting increasing diversity and fragmentation. This account of connectedness suggests the structural impact of distant decisions without specifying the impact.

Reading 1.4: Anthony Giddens

This piece explains diversity as fragmentation and touches on the different impacts of globalization on rich and poor.

WORKBOOK ACTIVITY 1.4

As a way of checking your understanding of terms and issues raised in this chapter, try to write brief notes on the following before checking your answers in the text.

The pessimistic view of globalization

Regionalization

Global infrastructure.

COMMENT

Discussions of these terms can be found in the chapter as follows: pessimistic view, p.22; regionalization, p.15; and global infrastructure, p.17.

Use this as an opportunity to reflect on how you got on and your reactions to the activity. It is quite possible that you felt rather irritated because you couldn't answer the question or that you tried but came up with wrong answers. This is particularly irritating if you believed you had read the chapter with interest and had generally understood what it was all about. Many people will be in the same position as yourself. Treat this as a learning process. You may need to think carefully about meaning as you are reading material and to *reflect* on what you are reading to ensure it makes sense to you.

After you have read a section in a chapter do spend a few minutes trying to recall the essentials of what it said; a few minutes active thinking in this way can save you hours of reading later when you come to revise material for assignments or (in later courses) examinations.

1.2 Globalization: concepts and evidence

In Section 3.1 of the chapter, Allan Cochrane and Kathy Pain specify four distinctive features of globalization. This is very important because it presents us with a list against which examples of globalization can be checked.

The four features identified were:

- *stretched* social relations
- *intensification* of flows and interactions
- *interpenetration* of global and local social processes
- the development of a transnational *infrastructure*.

These can be difficult concepts to grasp, but they are very important for your work in this block and so now is the best time to make sure that you fully understand them.

WORKBOOK ACTIVITY 1.5

In order to pick out the key features we have completed the following grid. Our version is on page 20. We've used Sections 3 and 5 from the chapter to fill in the first two columns and in order to focus on areas of doubt we thought of some counter arguments that indicate the world is becoming globalized. We also think that there are doubts about some of the evidence which has been put forward in support of the globalization argument.

We've included blank grids for you to have a go yourself before you have a look at our version, but don't worry if you prefer to go straight to the completed grid. See if you agree with our version.

	Meaning	Evidence	Areas of doubt
Stretched relations			
Intensification			

	Meaning	Evidence	Areas of doubt
Interpenetration			
Infrastructure			

C O M M E N T

Our completed grid is as follows.

	Meaning	Evidence	Areas of doubt
Stretched relations	Connections to and impact on distant places.	Examples of global pollution. More countries involved in international trade. Impact of communities in creating new shared social space.	Many people in developed countries still subsistence farmers. Internet usage, etc. still internationally patchy. Regionalization may be more important (EU, etc.).
Intensification	Fast speed of links and impact.	Rapid increase of electronic flows – satellite etc. Growth in international information.	Still do not directly involve most people, even in 'developed' world.
Interpenetration	Integration of local places – local affects global and vice versa.	Global role of Microsoft, McDonald's. 'Indian' restaurants in Britain. Brazilian soaps on Portuguese TV.	Do these seriously affect people's lives? Are they just added on to traditional routine?
Infrastructure	Old state controls no longer relevant or effective.	Role of new information and new technology.	Could states reassert control if they wished?

1.3 Theories of globalization

Section 4 of Chapter 1 introduced you to the three key positions in social science debates on globalization.

The debates over the significance of globalization will be developed in the other chapters of the book; each chapter will focus on a particular subject – culture and communications, the economy, and politics. And the authors of each chapter will be stressing different interpretations of globalization. Hugh Mackay will generally stress the globalist position (Chapter 2), Grahame Thompson the traditionalist view (Chapter 3), and Anthony McGrew the transformationalist interpretation (Chapter 4).

However, to make the most of those chapters you need to establish a solid foundation of understanding now.

WORKBOOK ACTIVITY 1.6

Look back to your notes on Section 4 of Chapter 1 and try filling in the grid below which draws on our four key questions. For each question, what view does a globalist, a traditionalist, and a transformationalist take?

	Globalists	Traditionalists	Transformationalists
What is globalization?			
How significant is contemporary globalization?			

	Globalists	Traditionalists	Transformationalists
What is the impact of globalization on the sovereignty and autonomy of nation-states?			
Are there winners and losers in globalization?			

COMMENT

	Globalists	Traditionalists	Transformationalists
What is globalization?	Real and tangible shift with social processes operating on a global level. An inevitable pattern producing a single global culture and economy, and reducing state sovereignty and autonomy.	An account that tends to ignore continuities with the past. It fails to recognize scope for state sovereignty and autonomy, and that most international economic and social activity is regional rather than global.	Globalization is a complex, diverse and unpredictable process which certainly has important effects but does not remove the scope of states for independent action.
How significant is contemporary globalization?	Very significant and far-reaching.	No fundamental changes are taking place.	Significant but patchy and difficult to quantify.
What is the impact of globalization on the sovereignty and autonomy of nation-states?	State sovereignty and autonomy are disappearing with a new global structure dominating.	States remain able to determine their own priorities and systems of governance.	States remain powerful but have to adjust their role in the face of new global corporations, etc.
Are there winners and losers in globalization?	Positive globalists see the potential for all to benefit from an improved quality of life. Pessimistic globalists see dominant groups imposing their agendas and interests on the rest.	A danger of global business imposing its priorities and increasing global inequalities – the weak and poor could lose further ground to the rich and powerful.	Some scope for all to benefit from a more democratic system of governance, but the unpredictability of the process could result in a complex pattern of winners and losers.

 Now please listen to Audio-cassette 7, Side A and read the associated notes. Then return to this point in the workbook.

2 THE GLOBALIZATION OF CULTURE?

Chapter 1 of *A Globalizing World?* introduced you to the key concepts for defining globalization and the key theories that try and explain its origins and consequences. The chapter also looked at the range of evidence we might use to evaluate these theories. Chapter 2 draws upon all of this but focuses on one area of social life – culture and communications. Within this enormous field its main concern is with television, although it draws on other cultural flows as well. Three core sections (Sections 2–4) look at how each of the positions on globalization interpret the impact of global flows of television on national and local cultures, government and policy making, and local and national identities. A range of different types of evidence is drawn upon in exploring these arguments and provides a good opportunity for practising the skills of handling and evaluating evidence which builds on the skills work in *Workbook 2* and *Study Skills Supplement 2: Reading Evidence.*

The chapter combines discussion of technologies (TV transmission systems) with cultural products (TV programmes) and concludes by looking at the relative importance of technologies and cultural products in shaping and determining the impact of globalization.

KEY TASKS

Chapter 2, 'The Globalization of Culture?'

- Understanding how our concepts of globalization can be applied to cultures and cultural flows.

- Understanding what account the three theories of globalization give of cultural change.

- Beginning to compare, contrast and evaluate the three accounts.

- Working on the presentation and handling of evidence.

- Exploring the *coherence* of theoretical arguments.

- Locating theories of globalization within larger political ideologies.

Now please read Chapter 2, 'The Globalization of Culture?' and then return to this point in the workbook. You should spend two-thirds of your time on the chapter and one-third on the workbook.

2.1 Extracting the key points from Chapter 2

The chapter stresses what it calls the 'phenomenal growth in the global circulation ... of cultural goods' over recent decades, offering data on:

- the extent of cultural imports and exports,

- the growth in ownership of TV receivers and radios, and

- the expansion in the number of television channels, cable and satellite broadcasting.

The key, however, is how these developments are interpreted, and Hugh Mackay summarizes the interpretations of the *positive* and *pessimistic globalizers*, the *traditionalists* and the *transformationalists*.

WORKBOOK ACTIVITY 2.1

If you have already made notes on the views of *optimistic globalists* and *pessimistic globalists* then compare them with ours. If not, put down, side-by-side, notes on the points raised by each of them.

Optimistic globalists	Pessimistic globalists

COMMENT

Our notes were as follows (as with all notes we would, in practice, have used shorthand and abbreviations).

Optimistic globalists	Pessimistic globalists
The idea of a 'global village' – allowing communities to develop across physical boundaries – McLuhan.	Growing inequalities – many people do not have access to information and communications.
Democratic and participatory nature of the Internet.	Media increasingly owned by fewer people, e.g. Murdoch – anti-democratic potential.
Space free from state control – this counters the powers of advertising, PR, etc. – Rheingold – now many voices can be heard.	Lower quality programming to cater for mass audience.
Use of Internet by opponents of a political system, minority ethnic group, etc. gives consumers freedom of choice.	Internet likely to develop in ways that suit major corporations. Cultural imperialism – threat to vulnerable cultures – dominance of US culture – Frankfurt School.

Note that we have included several names of theorists who have expressed particular views (e.g. McLuhan) and examples to illustrate points (e.g. Murdoch) for use in supporting arguments in an essay. An alternative would have been to put a page reference to the chapter so that we could look up the particular example/reference when needed.

WORKBOOK ACTIVITY 2.2

Now read through your notes on Sections 3 and 4 which cover the traditionalists and the transformationalists. Make a list of the key points of the *transformationalist* view in a 'bullet point' format. We will do this for the traditionalists.

COMMENT

Our key points of the *traditionalist* view:

- do accept some changes have taken place
- believe claims excessive with key cultural forms and institutions still national

- globalists overstate external structural forces vs. local dynamics
- BBC still more viewers than satellite and cable
- very little 'truly global' TV – MTV and Disney
- 1997 top 40 programmes in UK all domestically produced
- BSkyB in many ways a UK company
- globally, broadcast material which is domestically produced is 29 times greater than cross-border (O'Regan)
- UK press essentially domestically produced
- CNN has limited significance as a broadcaster
- still significant state means of regulation, e.g. 1990 Broadcasting Act.

There is a difficult balance to be drawn between brevity and full use of examples. Here we have reminders of prominent examples, but also we have made notes from material in the order in which it was presented in the chapter; we know just where to look up further examples if needed.

Now let's use these short notes and our readings to try and summarize the arguments of the chapter based on our four block questions.

WORKBOOK ACTIVITY 2.3

Try filling in the grid below and compare it with ours.

	Optimistic globalists	Pessimistic globalists	Traditionalists	Transformationalists
What is cultural globalization?				
How significant is contemporary cultural globalization?				
What is the impact on national cultures, identities and politics?				

	Optimistic globalists	Pessimistic globalists	Traditionalists	Transformationalists
Are there winners and losers in cultural globalization?				
Evidence used.				

COMMENT

	Optimistic globalists	Pessimistic globalists	Traditionalists	Transformationalists
What is cultural globalization?	The creation of new opportunities for people to participate in the free exchange of ideas and information, free from state control.	The concentration of the power to spread ideas into the hands of a few global corporations or dominant groups who can swamp minority cultures.	There is the potential for ideas and information to spread globally, but the nation-state remains the main regulatory body and the national press and TV remains dominant.	Global cultural flows are increasing but their actual significance is difficult to measure.
How significant is contemporary cultural globalization?	Highly significant.	Highly significant.	Of little significance	Potentially significant but unpredictable and requiring further study
What is the impact on national cultures, identities and politics?	Enriching and democratizing.	Swamping minority cultures and homogenizing	Marginal and peripheral.	Potentially significant but variable and unpredictable.
Are there winners and losers in cultural globalization?	Potentially all are winners	Global corporations and dominant Western cultures are the winners, while minority cultures are the losers	The weak are potentially the losers if pressure towards globalization is not checked	The pattern is complex but there is scope for cultural minorities within nation-states to benefit.
Evidence used.	Quantitative data on information flows / Qualitative interpretations on use made of the Internet, etc.	Data on patterns of ownership of the media / Data on patterns of cultural flows.	Quantitative data on audience share, patterns of readership. / Historical evidence of effects of the telegraph.	Data on programme content / Qualitative evidence of the active role of recipients of messages

2.2 Examining the coherence of an argument

Now let's look at Section 5 of the chapter where Hugh Mackay explores the role of technology as a factor in social change. His argument is that new technologies are key components of cultural globalization but claims their impact is gradual rather than revolutionary and that while technologies constrain societies they are themselves shaped by society.

WORKBOOK ACTIVITY 2.4

Read through Section 5 and make notes on how he develops this argument.

COMMENT

The key points we noted were:

- the telegraph greatly increased the speed of communication
- this led to cable laying, international hysteria and honours for its inventor
- claims of its impact were excessive – world peace, etc.
- terms like *stone age, steam age* stress the effects of technology, but the impact of technology depends on how technology is used
- change as a result of social concerns, etc. – the perceived needs of the US Department of Defence.

In diagrammatic form his argument can be represented thus:

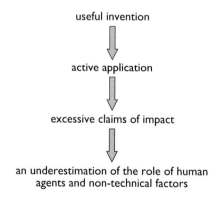

useful invention

active application

excessive claims of impact

an underestimation of the role of human
agents and non-technical factors

WORKBOOK ACTIVITY 2.5

The way Hugh Mackay presents this argument is coherent based on relevant facts and seems to be comprehensive in its coverage. Put yourself in the role of a critic, however, and see if you can identify any doubts or raise possible questions of his interpretation. Make a list of these for further consideration.

COMMENT _____

This is not an easy exercise, and doubtless Hugh Mackay would, if asked, present further justification of his views. However, we did note the following:

- He argues that the telegraph, not the Internet, was the real cause of the shrinking of time and space, but he then uses it to argue that claims about the telegraph were overblown. Could the logic of this chain of argument be questioned?

- Is there a precise parallel between the telegraph and the Internet? Could it be argued that many more people have got immediate access to the Internet than they did to the telegraph and therefore the speed of impact is likely to be different? Does the theory contain an unsustainable assumption? Has a possible line of reasoning been excluded without adequate consideration?

- Does the approach sufficiently take into account the argument that technologies may be social in their origin but can develop a momentum of their own?

Note that these points are not designed to dismiss Mackay's position, but merely to show that it is possible to raise questions and doubts about what appears a very persuasive argument.

2.3 Reading quantitative and diagrammatic evidence

One of the skills we want you to work on at this stage of the course is the critical evaluation of quantitative data, a great deal of which has been used in Chapter 2. The comments and activities here are designed to build on *Study Skills Supplement 2: Reading Evidence* and you may find it helpful to refer back to this now before proceeding with this workbook.

As we agreed in our discussion of crime in the Introductory Block, any set of statistics or tables of information have been compiled by people or institutions who may consciously or unconsciously ask questions, categorize responses/information, etc. into preconceived categories that may provide a partial or distorted picture of the world. It is therefore always important to note the sources of evidence and to consider whether the compiler or publisher might have some vested interest in the interpretations that can be drawn from the evidence; for example, the press in selling newspapers through sensationalism or politicians in showing the apparent effectiveness of their actions/policies.

Here the questions we want you to consider are rather different.

WORKBOOK ACTIVITY 2.6

Look again at Table 2.3 in the chapter which gives you information on changing patterns of television ownership in different nation-states. Try to identify and note significant information that the table does and does not tell you.

Think what extra information you would require before you could draw any conclusions about the impact of TV ownership on societies.

COMMENT

We will simply ask some questions to help you shape your answer:

● Does the extent of choice of channels matter?

● Is the source of programmes important?

● What alternatives are there to TV as cultural influences?

● How much time do people spend watching TV?

WORKBOOK ACTIVITY 2.7

Figure 4 shows exactly the same information that is presented in Table 2.3. By comparing the table and the figure we hope you can see the value of presenting evidence in different forms. Examine these two forms of presentation of data and make brief notes in answer to the question:

Do *you* think the key points can be more easily drawn from the figure or the table? In what ways?

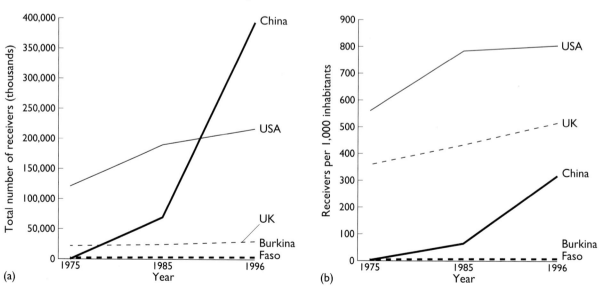

FIGURE 4   Television ownership and saturation in selected countries, 1975–96: (a) total number of receivers and (b) receivers per 1,000 inhabitants

Source: data in Table 2.3

C O M M E N T

Our thoughts are:

- Tables of numbers can appear to be complicated and rather off-putting.

- The figure helps you home in on the key point of the great increase of TV receivers in China but also that the number of receivers per 1,000 inhabitants in China is still, in 1996, considerably lower than in the USA.

- It is easier to obtain *precise* information from the table.

Whatever your reactions to this comparison it is always a useful exercise to test them against another example to see if this confirms them.

W O R K B O O K   ACTIVITY 2.8

Table 2.5 in the chapter gives information on the share of viewing time for public television corporations. Figure 5 shows the same information that is presented in the table. Compare Table 2.5 with Figure 5 and see if your reactions from the previous activity are confirmed.

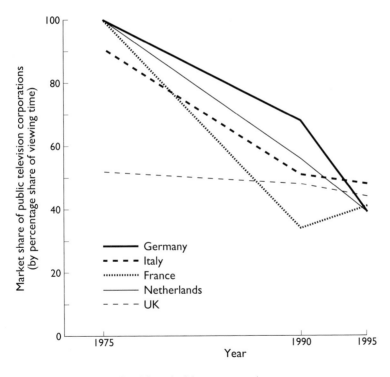

FIGURE 5   Market share of public television corporations

Source: data in Table 2.5

COMMENT

In this case we would suggest the points about relative clarity of message and the ability to produce precise statistics are even more justified, thus emphasizing the potential trade-off between the two requirements if only one form of presentation of data is to be used.

2.4 Theories of globalization and political ideologies

In Block 3 you were introduced to the key political ideologies of the post-Second World War UK. In Chapter 2, Hugh Mackay outlines a number of different views of global culture and communications under the headings of positive globalists, pessimistic globalists, traditionalists, and transformationalists. Is there any overlap? This section provides an opportunity for you to practise ideology-spotting skills.

WORKBOOK ACTIVITY 2.9

Look back at the material in Book 3 on Marxism and liberalism to remind yourself of their key assumptions (Chapter 4, pp.129–31 and pp.134–6). Then look again at your notes on the sections of Hugh Mackay's chapter that cover theories of globalization and see if you can identify any links between them.

Do this by completing the following grid. You may well find that parts of the grid will remain blank.

	Marxism	Liberalism
Positive globalists		

	Marxism	Liberalism
Pessimistic globalists		
Traditionalists		
Transformationalists		

C O M M E N T

	Marxism	Liberalism
Positive globalists		Belief in the value of the free market. Value free choice and diversity.
Pessimistic globalists	Growing inequalities within and between nations. Concentration of ownership – power of wealthy people and organizations. 'Western cultural imperialism' – to generate demand for goods.	
Traditionalists	Traditional patterns of power and inequality remain.	People have been given wider choice.
Transformationalists	There could be the development of three regional capitalist groups.	Culture is a two-way flow – imports fill less popular slots reflecting consumer choice. People 'localize' cultural messages.

Some of these points were easy to read off from the material available, while others required a more general understanding of the two traditions of thought. What the exercise shows, however, is that theories may be heavily influenced by traditions of thought/ideologies, but they do not neatly follow from them. As you can see, elements of the two ideologies could be found across a range of theories. Had we added conservatism, you would have found strong elements of this in the approaches of both the pessimistic globalists and the traditionalists.

 Now please listen to Audio-cassette 7, Side B and read the associated notes. Then return to this point in the workbook.

3 ECONOMIC GLOBALIZATION?

Chapter 2 looked at the globalization of culture. In Chapter 3 we want to 'drag you away from the television' and change the focus to theories of *economic globalization* and the extent to which the contemporary international economy can adequately be explained in those terms.

The chapter begins by trying to define the notion of economic globalization and then lays down some measures which will allow you to assess the accuracy of the economic globalization thesis. Another important point to look out for when reading Chapter 3 is the role of historical evidence in helping you to reach an assessment of the significance of contemporary developments. Just as we can reach conclusions about the significance of a modern 'crime wave' and the imminent breakdown of law and order by looking critically at a 'golden age' of social peace and harmony (*Introductory Chapter*, Section 3), so we can test the globalization thesis by looking at the nature and extent of international economic links in the past in comparison with present-day patterns.

KEY TASKS

Chapter 3, 'Economic Globalization?'

- To explore precise conceptual definitions of economic globalization.

- To understand the accounts of economic globalization provided by *globalists, traditionalists* and *transformationalists.*

- To work with a range of evidence on international trade and investment, critically evaluating its worth.

- To use that evidence to evaluate competing theoretical accounts of economic globalization.

Now please read Chapter 3, 'Economic Globalization?' and then return here. You should spend around two-thirds of your time on the chapter and one-third on the workbook.

3.1 Deciphering terminology

Debates about the nature and extent of economic globalization are ongoing, and we hope you found the contents of this chapter both interesting and informative, even though some of the concepts and examples were quite complex. Many of these ideas may well be new to you, so it is perhaps not surprising that even when greatly simplified, many of the arguments will still involve difficult phrases, etc. Hopefully, we have anticipated some of the problems you may have faced, so compare your understanding with the points below.

WORKBOOK ACTIVITY 3.1

Without looking up the terms in the chapter, briefly note down what you understand by the following terms:

- multinational corporations
- foreign direct investment
- gross domestic product
- Triad integration.

COMMENT

Multinational corporations (MNCs) are defined by Grahame Thompson as ones that have 'at least some productive capacity located abroad'. He suggests that in contrast with *transnational corporations (TNCs)*, MNCs do maintain a clear national base and are generally regulated by their 'home country' authorities. He gives the Pilkington glass company in the UK as an example.

Foreign direct investment involves the export of capital by MNCs or TNCs. Examples would be the establishment by Nissan of their car plant in Washington in the north-east of England or the results of a decision by, say, Pilkington to open a new manufacturing plant in Australia, or to buy a significant part of an Australian glass manufacturer.

Gross domestic product is a measure of the value of goods and services produced in a particular country in a specified period, usually a year. It would therefore include for the United Kingdom in the year 2000 the value of mining and agricultural production, manufactured goods and services (see also Book 2, Chapter 3, p.83).

Triad integration is based on the idea that there are essentially three trading blocs in the world; they are North America, the European Union and Japan. The extent of Triad integration therefore depends on the extent to which the three blocs have become mutually involved in trade and investment.

If you either couldn't give answers or you feel your answers were way off beam, don't feel too downcast. We selected these examples because we thought they were quite difficult terms (although you have come across GDP already in Book 2) and the exercise was meant to illustrate a couple of key points.

In the first place, as we read through the material it is all too easy to lose focus and skate over terms that would otherwise give us problems. In terms of skimming material (see the *Introductory Workbook*) this is quite an understandable and sensible strategy as we are simply trying to get the gist of the argument. However, if the material is central to the points being made in a piece of text then we need to reflect on our understanding of what is being said. We repeat – *at the end of a section, do ask yourself what it was essentially about and question yourself about any terms raised in it.*

The activity also raises one of the key problems of working alone: the possibility of facing difficulties in understanding such terms.

What should you do and not do in such circumstances?

Your answer will clearly depend on the extent of the problem; if there are many problems of understanding then your strategy will be very different from a situation in which there are only two or three points of difficulty. All we can do here is offer you a checklist with some comments:

- **Panic, feel inadequate, cry, provoke an argument with your 'nearest and dearest', kick the cat, etc.** All, with the exception of animal abuse, are understandable reactions, but not realistic solutions, often causing more problems than they can solve. Academic study is hard work, and every student has difficulties understanding material from time to time. You need to develop the confidence to accept this and find ways of living with it.

- **Telephone someone.** Your tutor is an obvious candidate for this, although telephone calls every hour can cause even the most mild-mannered and supportive tutor to develop a nervous tic, or contemplate emigration! Other students are a valuable resource here, and spreading calls around several members of a self-help group can lead to good, friendly working relationships. (On phoning your tutor, see *Workbook 1*, p.63.)

- **Using a dictionary, reference book, etc.** This can be helpful, although as you have probably already noticed, social scientists often use terms in specialized ways that a conventional dictionary may not deal with. Specialist 'Dictionaries of Social Science' exist, but often go deeply into the origins and varied usages of a term. This can leave you even more confused than when you started.

- **Battle away.** Reading the passage(s) many times so that the meaning eventually becomes clear. This can work and is certainly worth trying if the problems are few. However, a great deal of time can be wasted if too many terms are involved. Early in your studies this may be difficult, but it is important to use your judgement here. If a term appears several times or seems to be at the core of the writer's argument, then persevere. If it is only briefly referred to and does not seem to be central, then note it down and delay action on it until it either appears again or you get the opportunity at a tutorial or during a telephone call to seek clarification.

3.2 Extracting the key points from Chapter 3

The chapter highlights the relevance of globalization debates to economic policy and developments by pointing to the speed and extent of the impact that the financial crisis in East Asia had on both the United Kingdom and the rest of the world: factories closing, currencies losing their value, etc. As Grahame Thompson puts it, the 'web of interconnectedness between economies was linking external events to internal ones on an unprecedented global scale'.

The key to this chapter, however, is Thompson's claim that the globalization thesis has been greatly over-stated, and this he explicitly argues from the *traditionalist* position.

WORKBOOK ACTIVITY 3.2

Skim your notes on the chapter and jot down the basic points Thompson makes to justify his traditionalist and sceptical position in the debate.

COMMENT _____

We have chosen to put these points under a clear sub-heading of 'Reasons for scepticism' and in a bullet list format because the points are likely to be separate and distinct rather than flowing into a single argument. The list format should more effectively help us to remember how many points there were and their distinctiveness.

REASONS FOR SCEPTICISM

- Lack of a clearly defined concept of globalization.
- Capacity of the term to 'inflate', to cover ever-widening features of life: economics, culture, technology, crime, development, etc.
- Scattered examples do not necessarily constitute a pattern; the literature of globalization has taken them out of context.
- Arguments are a mishmash of analysis of economic processes and cultural and social development.

Thompson is essentially arguing that both the idea of globalization and the theories built up around it are vague, imprecise and lack coherence; that the available evidence does not support them; and that whatever their value in interpreting culture or political change their comprehensiveness does not stretch to the economic domain; that is, they are found wanting on our three tests used to evaluate theories (see the introduction to this workbook on the three tests).

Thompson outlines the globalist, traditionalist and transformationalist positions on the changing global economy, and then produces what he calls 'a working definition of economic globalization' (Section 3). He regards this as an essential task to be conducted before the accuracy of the competing approaches can be tested.

WORKBOOK ACTIVITY 3.3

Note down the key elements of the definition of economic globalization that Thompson produces.

COMMENT

Simply re-writing his definition will be of limited help. If you are to understand his ideas, it is essential to identify the important elements in your own words. Our response would be as follows:

- increased trade across the globe
- greater movement of finance and technical knowledge
- the removal of the independence of any country's economy
- the growing importance of companies that produce and trade internationally.

Another key issue to clarify before we can begin to analyse Thompson's view is the question of how to measure the extent of globalization, which he raises in Sections 4 and 5 (compare with the debate on evidence in Chapter 1, Section 5). Much of this material may be new to you and the use of new terminology and statistical data can be off-putting. It is, however, important to grasp these ideas if you are going to be able to understand and evaluate arguments about economic globalization. Take your time with it and read through it several times if necessary.

WORKBOOK ACTIVITY 3.4

Note down what measures Thompson selects of economic globalization, why he chooses them, and how he expresses them.

COMMENT

He identifies *trade flows* and *capital flows* as the key indicators of the extent of economic globalization.

However, he rejects the idea of simply measuring the increase in global trade because such data might only reflect increased total trade resulting from increased wealth. In other words, if we buy more imported clothes it might be:

(a) because for whatever reason we prefer them, or have to buy them, instead of UK-produced clothes and we are simply substituting the one for the other,

or

(b) our income has risen and we are buying more imported clothes in addition to more UK-produced clothes.

In this example reason (a) would be evidence of globalization while reason (b) would not, although it would indicate an increase in global trade.

As a result, Thompson prefers to measure changes in global trade by expressing trade as a fraction or ratio of output. So in the case of (b) above if the increase in trade simply reflects the increase in income the fraction or ratio would remain the same.

Similarly, and for the same reasons, he measures long-term capital flows in terms of foreign direct investment (FDI) as a ratio of GDP rather than just accepting the basic figures on increased investment.

3.3 Practice with numbers

The use of statistical evidence in this chapter provides an ideal opportunity to practise number skills, and indeed we are given a number of examples of calculations involving ratios and percentages from the material presented. Here we want to provide the opportunity for you to check your understanding of what is being done and to help you work through a few more examples.

Let's begin by looking in general at measuring rates of growth.

When we want to analyse how things change over time we are not interested in the absolute change in the value of, say, exports between two dates, but in the relative significance of the change. For example, the fact that the exports of a firm have increased by £500,000 is much more significant if the firm's previous level of exports was £1,000,000 rather than £10,000,000. In the first case there would be a very large increase of exports compared to a marginal increase in the second case.

	Case 1	Case 2
Previous year's exports (£)	1,000,000	10,000,000
Increase in exports for year in question (£)	500,000	500,000
Exports for year in question (£)	1,500,000	10,500,000

Comparing the change of a value or quantity to its initial size gives valuable information about the speed of change, so we calculate rates of growth.

Using a simple formula we have:

$$\text{rate of growth in exports} = \frac{\text{growth in exports}}{\text{previous level of exports}}$$

The growth in exports simply equals exports in the year in question minus exports in the previous year. So in the first case mentioned above the growth in exports (expressed in pounds) is £1,500,000 – £1,000,000 = £500,000.

The rate of growth expressed as a percentage is therefore:

$$\frac{500,000}{1,000,000} \times \frac{100}{1} = 50 \text{ per cent.}$$

WORKBOOK ACTIVITY 3.5

Now, calculate the rate of growth for the second case mentioned above, noting that the previous value of exports had been £10,000,000.

COMMENT

In this case the growth in exports is again 500,000, obtained by subtracting 10,000,000 from 10,500,000.

So growth in exports = 500,000.

The rate of growth expressed as a percentage is:

$$\text{rate of growth in exports} = \frac{\text{growth in exports}}{\text{previous level of exports}}$$

$$= \frac{500,000}{10,000,000} \times \frac{100}{1} = 5 \text{ per cent.}$$

Now let's look at some calculations drawn from material in the chapter. Look again at the paragraphs on GDP in Section 4.1, 'Trade and GDP' before proceeding.

WORKBOOK ACTIVITY 3.6

Work through the following examples and then check your answers with ours in the accompanying comments. Feel free to use a calculator here, and you should certainly do so for question 2 onwards.

1   A country in a particular year had a GDP of £500 million and trade of £100 m. What is:

(a) its trade to GDP ratio?

(b) the percentage of GDP produced by trade?

2   In 1998 a country exported £455 m worth of goods, and in 1999 £623 m worth of goods. Assuming the value of the pound remained constant, by what percentage had the value of its exports increased?

3   Using the same example and figures, but assuming an inflation rate of the pound of 10 per cent, by what percentage had the value of its exports now increased?

4   In 1999 the GDP of a country was £213,502 m and its merchandise trade was £27,105 m. What was its merchandise trade to GDP ratio, expressed as a percentage?

C O M M E N T

1   (a) The trade to GDP ratio is 100:500 which equals 1:5. (The ratio in the chapter is in the form of 100/500 or 1/5.)

(b) The percentage is £100m/£500m × 100 which equals 20 per cent.

Note that in the chapter Grahame Thompson combined these two calculations together to produce his answer to a similar question (e.g. see Activity 3.1).

2   First,

$$623 - 455 = 168$$

which is the absolute growth in export value.

This increase in export value as a percentage is then:

$$\frac{168}{455} \times 100 = 36.92 \text{ per cent.}$$

3   The percentage increase is now 23.23 per cent.

This is worked out by:

- calculating 10 per cent of 623 = 62.3
- subtracting 62.3 from 623 to find the 1999 exports at 1998 prices = 560.7
- subtracting 455 from 560.7 to find the increased value of exports = 105.7
- dividing 105.7 by 455 and multiplying by 100 = 23.230769
- correcting the figure to two decimal places = 23.23

4   The ratio as a percentage is 12.7 per cent.

The ratio is 27,105:213,502 and the percentage is obtained by multiplying by 100, that is:

$$\frac{27,105}{213,502} \times 100 = 12.695431 \text{ per cent.}$$

The result becomes 12.70 per cent when corrected to two decimal places.

If you haven't tackled anything like this before then you should not be too horrified if you found it quite challenging. If you can't follow the exercise then don't give up – other students will probably be in the same situation so ask your tutor if they will work through some simpler examples with you in a tutorial or on the telephone, etc.

3.4 An evaluation of the traditionalist view

In the conclusion to his chapter (Section 8), Grahame Thompson argues that there is a sceptical traditionalist view of globalization which is worth taking seriously. The points made in support of this argument are:

- globalization is at best an uneven process;

- it mainly affects short-term capital movements which could be regulated, although this would be a difficult process and require considerable political will;

- the international economy has changed in many ways but it can be argued that it is not as 'globalized' at the end of the twentieth century as it was in 1913;

- the international economy is still managed, and more could be done if there were the political will to do so; and

- states remain important actors in an 'internationalized' economy.

We certainly found this argument very persuasive. It links together in a logical and *coherent* way, and musters a wealth of *evidence* in support of it. The account is also *comprehensive*, taking into consideration world trade figures, regional trade flows, trade with developing countries, etc.

However, we want to use it as an example of how an argument or theory can be evaluated. Grahame Thompson is keen to point out that what he has presented in the chapter is not a fully fleshed-out theory because he is not trying to establish a definite pattern of cause and effect – he is merely producing evidence that casts doubt on the claims that there is a globalized economy and so he is associating himself with the essentials of the traditionalist position. Nevertheless, we want to use what he has written to show how the tests of a theory can be applied and to use the points raised in the introduction of this workbook.

This is an important activity to engage in now as the evaluation of a theory is the essence of the TMA question you will be answering at the end of this block.

WORKBOOK ACTIVITY 3.7

Read through the chapter again and note down, or underline, any points of information in it that might be used to question or cast doubts on the accuracy of the conclusion.

COMMENT _____

What we are doing here is to use the criteria of *coherence, empirical adequacy* and *comprehensiveness* to critically assess an argument. It is probable that satisfactory responses to many, if not all, of the questions or doubts raised below can be produced by Grahame Thompson; but at this stage some of the points we would begin with are as follows.

- The early admission that a financial crisis in one part of the world had rapid and extensive repercussions throughout the globe.

- Disagreement over definitions of globalization. As the chapter acknowledges, it could be that the particular definition selected determines the answer to the question.

- It is argued that there 'may be only instances and no phenomenon' of globalization. It may be that critics would read the evidence differently.

- The chapter argues that MNCs can be, and many are, 'effectively monitored, regulated and policed by "home country" authorities'. It could, however, be counter-argued that some of these companies have so much financial clout and the ability to move significant elements of their productive activities, etc. elsewhere, that their potential power to avoid regulation is considerable (e.g. Rupert Murdoch's relationship with the Blair government in the late 1990s? – compare with the discussion of Murdoch in Chapter 2, Section 2.3).

- The chapter suggests that there are relatively few examples of truly footloose TNCs; the question may then be asked as to whether their numbers are expanding or likely to do so in the future.

- It is acknowledged that the use of 'current prices' to measure the degree of trade openness arguably leads to an underestimate of the real growth of trade.

- Similarly, if figures for merchandise production were substituted for GDP, then again figures more sympathetic to the globalist view would be produced.

- It could be argued that evidence for 'trilateral regionalization' is as critical of the traditionalist position as it is of the globalist one.

Having identified possible points to use, where then do *coherence, empirical adequacy* and *comprehensiveness* come in? Taking a highly critical position, the questions or doubts raised could be grouped in the following way:

- *Coherence*

   Some of the issues mentioned above can be used to test the coherence of the argument. How coherent is it to admit that the East Asian crisis had rapid and far-reaching effects and then to suggest globalization is 'a literature of anecdote, inference and reliance on the accumulation of isolated facts'? Is it coherent to dismiss globalization in favour of the traditionalist view, but then to present evidence favouring a regionalization approach? Have the chosen definitions of globalization shaped the conclusions reached and excluded other possible arguments?

- *Empirical adequacy*

  The example of the Asian financial crisis could again be raised here. Does the approach adequately take into account the actual and potential powers of MNCs? Has the chapter ignored relevant evidence such as the extent to which the 'developing South' is indebted to and therefore potentially subject to the 'developed North'? What is the evidence that 'home country' authorities effectively police the activities of MNCs?

- *Comprehensiveness*

  The analysis has concentrated on trade and long-term capital flows. Is the argument able to take account of the growth in global services such as banking, tourism and, most importantly, information processing? Can an emphasis on financial value adequately measure the extent of possible integrating effects of global cultural transmissions?

These points are not raised to establish the accuracy or inaccuracy of this particular view. They are merely an illustration of how a critic of a particular theory would raise questions and doubts about it. The argument of any chapter in DD100 could have been treated in this way. As we have indicated, it is highly likely that a defender of the view could respond to each point, either to dismiss it as misguided or to offer further evidence to support her or his view. For example, it could be argued that our final criticism of the argument – failing to measure integrating effects of cultural transmission – is unfair given the explicit focus on the chapter on *economic* globalization.

We will examine Anthony McGrew's views on the *transformationalist* interpretation of globalization and the state in the next section in a similar way.

 Now please listen to Audio-cassette 8, Side A and read the associated notes. Then return to this point in the workbook.

4 POWER SHIFT: FROM NATIONAL GOVERNMENT TO GLOBAL GOVERNANCE?

This chapter focuses on recent developments in the relationship between nation-states and the inter-state system, examining in particular the changing relationships between the United Kingdom and wider international political institutions and influences. It begins by showing how a local event – the death of a young person from an overdose of heroin – can only be understood within a global context.

The chapter highlights the transformationalist position, essentially arguing that while power is no longer primarily located on a national scale, the nation-state continues to have an important role in global governance.

KEY TASKS

Chapter 4, 'Power Shift: From National Government to Global Governance?'

- To answer the question, 'is politics becoming globalized?' and to explore the transformationalist account of globalization.

- To understand the concept of 'global governance'.

- To examine how global governance is being conducted and in whose interests.

- To explore whether we are entering a more unruly or benign world order.

- To critically evaluate the transformationalist argument.

Now read Chapter 4, 'Power Shift: From National Government to Global Governance?' and then return here. You should spend two-thirds of your time on the chapter and one-third on the workbook.

4.1 Extracting the key points from Chapter 4

In this chapter Anthony McGrew is essentially contrasting a past era of global politics dominated by nation-states (what he refers to as the *Westphalian system*) with a developing pattern of politics in the contemporary era that he calls *multi-layered global governance*. In Activity 4.4 in Section 4 of the chapter he asked you to complete a grid which contrasts what he calls the *Westphalian Ideal* with the *Post-Westphalian system*. Before we can begin to evaluate his argument we must first be clear what he means by these concepts and so here we want to make sure you have fully grasped the points he is making.

The Treaty of Westphalia (1648) put an end to the Thirty Years War which was a complex mixture of religious wars, state and empire building, and local class conflicts mainly fought on the territory that is now modern Germany. Without getting involved in the intricacies of the war, it is important to note that it resulted in a defeat for the pretensions of the Emperor of Austria who had hoped to exercise authority over wide swathes of Europe in the name of the 'Holy Roman Emperor' – a title dating back to Charlemagne and the year AD 800. Simultaneously, the war saw the rise of individual princes with the authority to rule over their own small states and to determine the official religions of their populations free from external interference. The system that has come to govern the relationships between these kinds of sovereign states is the Westphalian system.

Five key features of the Westphalian system were identified in Chapter 4:

- territoriality
- sovereignty
- autonomy
- primacy
- anarchy.

WORKBOOK ACTIVITY 4.1

Refer again to Sections 2.1 and 4 of the chapter and then make sure that you have attempted to complete the table in Activity 4.4 which is reproduced below.

	Westphalian Ideal	Post-Westphalian system
Territoriality		

	Westphalian Ideal	Post-Westphalian system
Sovereignty		
Autonomy		
Primacy		
Anarchy		

COMMENT

Now compare your responses with ours.

	Westphalian Ideal	Post-Westphalian system
Territoriality	Legal and pol. powers of state limited to terr. borders	Borders important – but don't define limits of pol. life and community
Sovereignty	Sov. absolute moral and legal right of states	State power redefined – sov. is a bargaining tool, being bartered, shared and divided
Autonomy	State's right to self-determination and non-interference	State autonomy compromised by interdependence
Primacy	No higher auth. than state – rels. between states depend on consent or force	Primacy, legal and moral challenged
Anarchy	Interstate pol. has dominant power, pol. is free-for-all	Sharing of pol. – McGrew calls it heterarchy, p.163 Erosion of division between dom. and intern.

We have tried to indicate where we would have used abbreviations but have attempted to make them understandable to you by making the words longer than just for personal use. Where we wanted to be sure of the correct spelling of a technical term that we might wish to use in an assignment (namely, heterarchy) we have written it in full and named the source so that we can be sure of the accuracy of the representation.

Anthony McGrew's analysis is built on the *transformationalist* argument, that much more change has taken place in the global sphere than *traditionalists* allow; but it rejects the *globalist* view as too extreme. Essentially McGrew is arguing that the state retains an important role in the global system, even if the role has changed dramatically by comparison to the past.

In Section 2.2 he builds up the argument that global politics is having a significant impact on the UK.

WORKBOOK ACTIVITY 4.2

Make short notes of Section 2.2 and then compare them with ours below.

C O M M E N T

Our notes were:

- 'all areas of human activity' move across terr. boundaries
- nation-states are now 'spaces permeated' by global flows and networks
- power is being internationalized
- G8 - no country can itself stop the drugs trade, or make its own decisions on taxation, the environment, etc
- connects. of gov. depts with international bodies
- 'explosive' growth of intern. bodies - tenfold since 1909
- numerous intern. confs
- growth of intern. NGOs and networks
- the 'institutionalization' of transnational networks
- new centres of authority 'above, below and alongside the state'
- growing 'infrastructure of transnational civil society'
- govts accept wider controls and interests, eg EU, WTO

In Section 2.3 McGrew argues there are institutions of global governance that can be identified at three levels: the *suprastate*, the *substate*, and the *transnational*, with the layer of national government 'sandwiched' between them.

WORKBOOK ACTIVITY 4.3

Read through Section 2.3 and complete the following grid.

	Evidence of institutions of global governance
Suprastate layer	

Evidence of institutions of global governance

Substate layer	
Transnational layer	

C O M M E N T

We have completed our version of the first row to show again the use of abbreviations, examples, etc.

Evidence of institutions of global governance
Suprastate layer

Suprastate layer: *Large no. of new intern. bodies, eg WTO. They are new: legal identity with pension schemes etc, wide membership and responsibilities.*

Emergence of reg. groupings and global alliances.

Frequent and substantive summits, ie they take decisions and make policy.

Intern. bodies shape domestic policy, eg corp. pun.

Conflicts often reflect functions rather than nationality, eg finance.

W O R K B O O K A C T I V I T Y 4.4

Read again through Sections 2.4 and 3.3 of the chapter and note down the key points made in support of the transformationalist case.

C O M M E N T

Many points could have been noted, ours were:

- state still important but no longer a 'container' – rather a 'space of flows'
- national politics now embedded in wider 'communities of fate'
- shifting balance of power between states and global markets, e.g. East Asian crash
- the transformationalist approach recognizes the importance of individual agents in governance
- 'network' politics resist the forces of global capitalism, thereby leading to elements of 'governance from below', e.g. the 'Stop the MAI' campaign
- important role of experts, at the expense of citizens and politicians, in coping with systemic risks
- the transformationalist position recognizes the significance of state power, corporate power and people power.

To represent the transformationalist argument diagrammatically:

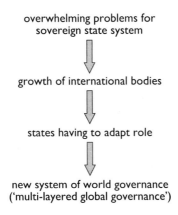

4.2 Evaluating the transformationalist argument

In previous sections of this workbook we have raised questions/doubts about aspects of the arguments presented by Hugh Mackay and Grahame Thompson to show how a critic might begin to evaluate a theory. Now let us have a go at evaluating Anthony McGrew's analysis. Here we will approach McGrew's argument from a *traditionalist* position.

Let's start by focusing on the above diagram which summarizes McGrew's transformationalist views and see what questions/doubts we can raise.

WORKBOOK ACTIVITY 4.5

Think carefully about each of the links in the chain in the diagram and try to come up with questions that could be raised about them from the *traditionalist* view.

COMMENT

The questions we would raise:

- *Are the problems facing states so much more overwhelming than those in the past?* Major international threats to the existence of states pre-date the Second World War: the great plagues such as the Black Death; invaders such as the Vikings, Napoleon, or Nazi Germany; internal divisions (Royalists vs. Roundheads, nineteenth- and twentieth-century revolutionary movements, Irish nationalism); and international piracy; etc.

- *Are international bodies simply a response to problems or do they merely reflect new ways of pursuing a narrow national interest?* Membership of the World Trade Organization has enabled the USA to push the interests of US owners of banana plantations etc. These international organizations can be said to serve rather than displace the interests of particular states.

- *Are states really adapting their role to such an extent?* They are at least as powerful as ever in policing their populations: they control immigration; they imprison, tax, and mobilize their citizens into armed forces when necessary; and they still take on the responsibilities for the health and education of their populations.

- *Is there really evidence of a new pattern of world governance?* The UN and its agencies can only act when the dominant powers are in agreement; intervention takes place only when the stronger states decide to act in relation to weaker ones (Kosovo, East Timor) and not when the interests of stronger ones are threatened (Russia with regard to Chechnya, China in the case of Tibet). The pattern may not be that states are getting weaker but that new ones are emerging (Croatia, Slovakia and possibly Catalonia, Scotland, etc.). It needs to be stressed that changing boundaries and the creation of new entities has always characterized the Westphalian system (e.g. Belgium, Germany and Italy in the nineteenth century).

So let's take these, and any other questions/doubts we have, and apply the tests of *coherence, empirical adequacy*, and *comprehensiveness* to the transformationalist argument.

Coherence. Again it is possible that answers can be provided by *transformationalists* to these questions, but there are several which can be raised:

- Is it logical to admit that the world campaign against slavery and the slave trade occurred over a century ago and yet still to argue that globalization is new?

- Is it logical to talk about the inability of the state to be sovereign and yet to conclude that 'great inequalities of power, access and influence exist'? Would this not simply support the traditionalist case that at different historical periods there may be different dominant powers?

- Similarly, in terms of NGOs, Anthony McGrew points out that 'many of the poorest and most vulnerable members of the world community have no effective voice at all', does this not again offer support for the traditionalist position?

- Is it logical to assume that states will be willing to accept adapted roles and that new patterns of governance will emerge? Are there unsustainable assumptions of inevitability contained in this argument?

Empirical adequacy. The chapter certainly mobilizes a great deal of evidence in support of its contentions, but there are pieces of evidence that do not fit in:

- Some states have rejected moves towards joining regional groupings, for example Norway and Switzerland rejecting EU membership.

- How representative and significant are the NGOs? What relevance did the Beijing Women's Forum have to the people of Bangladesh and Burkina

Faso, or even to attitudes and behaviour in the Midwest of the USA or Sicily?

- How effective have international organizations, of whatever sort, been in preventing the continued burning of rain forests in Indonesia or Central America?

- Does the evidence offer satisfactory explanations for the rise of nationalism in East Timor, Chechnya or Croatia?

Comprehensiveness. From the points on empirical adequacy we can cast doubts on the approach's ability to explain every example, but in addition we can suggest:

- Does it adequately take into account the strength of the USA, and perhaps a few other states, to dominate international organizations and produce changes that are in its (their) own interests? Is it a model that works for small- and medium-sized states, but not for superpowers?

WORKBOOK ACTIVITY 4.6

Just spend a few minutes considering McGrew's argument from a *globalist* position and try to identify three questions or doubts that its supporters might raise about the *transformationalist* argument. Try to raise a point for each of our three tests of a theory – *coherence, empirical adequacy* and *comprehensiveness*.

C O M M E N T

Possible points that came to our minds were:

- Membership of the EU has undoubtedly reduced the sovereignty of the British state in terms of the authority of its courts, its ability to place controls on trade. Is it *coherent* then to argue that state power is merely changing rather than being lost?

- Isn't the failure of states to deal with the international drug problem evidence that state power is a thing of the past and so the transformationalist view is not *empirically adequate*?

- Does the transformationalist position adequately take into account the power of MNCs to shape our consumption, attitudes and tastes via the Internet, mass media, advertising, etc? Is it therefore a *comprehensive* argument?

 Now please read *Study Skills Supplement 3: Reading Maps* and listen to the associated Audio-cassette 8, Side B. Then return to this point in the workbook.

5 REFLECTION AND CONSOLIDATION

As in previous blocks of the course, now is the opportunity to pause and consolidate your knowledge and understanding before launching into TMA 04.

 Now please read the Afterword to Book 4. Also watch TV 04 around now (depending on broadcast schedules) and read the associated notes.

Then return to this point in the workbook.

David Held's Afterword to *A Globalizing World?* has, we hope, given you a clearer sense of the debates around the four key questions of this block, as well as some reflection on the role of *structure and agency* in the globalization debate, the *diversity* of responses to globalization and the *uncertainties* it generates.

In Section 5.2 we will be returning to the core questions of the block and in Section 5.3 we look at the use of some of the course themes. But first we want to revisit some aspects of the key skill of the block – *evaluation*.

5.1 Evaluation revisited

You have already covered a lot of ground on evaluation. It is worth reflecting for a moment where in the workbook you have touched on this issue.

- The introduction, which looked at the place of evaluation in the circuit of knowledge and examined three items: *coherence, empirical adequacy* and *comprehensiveness.*

- Section 1.2 which identified four features of globalization which could be used to test propositions about it – these would effectively test the *empirical adequacy* of any theory of globalization.

- Section 1.3 where a grid summarized points raised by globalizers, traditionalists and transformationalists.

- Section 2.1 in which contrasts were drawn between the interpretations of the optimistic and pessimistic globalists.

- Section 2.2 which showed how the *coherence* of an argument could be questioned.

- Section 2.4 which showed how social science theories are linked to *larger schools of thought* and *ideologies.*

- Section 3.4 which outlined and offered a critical assessment of the *traditionalist* view.

- Section 4.2 which outlined and offered a critical assessment of the *transformationalist* point of view.

In addition to this we want to briefly address two further questions about evaluation (which we will return to in Block 5): the role of *social values* in shaping social science theories (see also *Workbook 3*, Section 2.4) and the ways in which theories can respond to evidence.

WORKBOOK ACTIVITY 5.1

Imagine that you are passing through a shopping precinct and you are hailed by someone selling copies of *The Big Issue*. Note down what you believe your assessment of the situation would be, and also try to think of how someone with different values from yourself might interpret it.

COMMENT

Some of us might feel that here is the homeless victim of an unequal and uncaring society who at least deserves the price of the magazine. To others, here is an irresponsible work-shy individual who has 'dropped out' of society, probably indulges in alcohol and/or drug abuse and who should not be allowed to be a virtual beggar on our streets. All of us would see the evidence of a poorly dressed and perhaps sickly-looking individual, but we then, as a result of our values, put a gloss on our interpretation. Therefore we can say that *the observer's values shape the interpretation of the evidence*.

The material we have read in this block has certainly shown that despite diligent and painstaking research, social scientists continue to disagree – in this case globalists vs. traditionalists vs. transformationalists. This further illustrates the point that evidence does not 'speak for itself' – it has to be both selected and interpreted, and our 'values' play an important role in these processes.

One important contribution to an understanding of the relationships between theories, evidence and values has been offered by Steven Lukes (1981, p.396) who has suggested that 'theories may be *underdetermined* by data'. By this he means that data or evidence are vital in the establishment of a theory, but data or evidence alone cannot determine a theory's accuracy because values also come into it. To put it another way, any theory is the product of both evidence and values, and consequently two contrasting theories may each fit the evidence. The figure below shows how evidence and values combine to produce a theory, and this, therefore, justifies the social science approach of identifying, collecting and debating evidence to challenge and require a reworking of any theory. This does not mean that the production of evidence will necessarily convert a proponent of one theory to support another, but it may require a reworking of any theory.

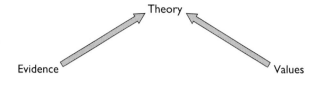

WORKBOOK ACTIVITY 5.2

Look back over the possible points of objection that we raised in Section 3 of this workbook (Workbook Activity 3.7) to Grahame Thompson's traditionalist theory. Note down some points on what you think his reaction would be if he were asked to comment.

COMMENT

What is definite is that he wouldn't throw in the towel and declare himself a convert to globalism! He would certainly reject many of the points made – indeed in the chapter itself he has already made a spirited defence of the definitions and measures he used. He might, however, take on board the need to defend his argument against potential critics – he might produce new and more comprehensive examples which the constraints of word limits did not allow him in the original text. He might clarify some statements to avoid misunderstanding or misinterpretation. He might even accept that a particular question or point of criticism has some validity and make a marginal change to his argument when he next presents it.

Indeed, you know this already at a rather different level from discussions you have had with your friends or loved ones – when they make a telling point in an argument, you don't immediately give in, but you do make a mental note to take on board the point so next time you argue your case you are not vulnerable to it and your argument is consequently stronger.

Do think about this next time you find yourself in a discussion and test whether our prediction of your behaviour is correct.

So that while evidence can disprove or require the reworking of a theory, no amount of evidence can *prove* it to be true. Moreover, we can never know what new evidence will come to light in the future that might totally discredit our apparently sound theory. For example, ancient Egyptians believed that the earth was the centre of the universe because all the visual evidence available to them supported this; the sun and moon and even the stars seemed to travel around it. They could not have predicted the invention of the telescope, etc. which would totally disprove this theory. All we can say is that *the greater the evidence amassed in favour of a particular theory, the stronger that theory will appear to be.*

5.2 Theories of globalization revisited

In Section 1 we began to develop a table of details on the key features of each of the theories of globalization. Here we want you to extend and complete this to provide yourself with a useful summary of the material for use in TMA 04 and also the final assignment of the course.

WORKBOOK ACTIVITY 5.3

Have a go at filling in this grid and compare it with ours below. We suggest you fill in the grid using chapter, section and page numbers from Book 4 so that you have a series of references that you can look up when preparing for TMA 04 or revising for TMA 06.

	Globalists	Traditionalists	Transformationalists
What is globalization?			
How significant is contemporary globalization?			

	Globalists	Traditionalists	Transformationalists
What is the impact of globalization on the sovereignty and autonomy of nation-states?			
Are there winners and losers in globalization?			
Evidence for			

	Globalists	Traditionalists	Transformationalists
Key evidence against			
Place of theory in wider political ideologies			

C O M M E N T _____

The use of page/section numbers rather than actual points has the benefit that
more references can be included. This works with OU courses because you
have ownership of the appropriate books and can easily look up references.
It would be of much more limited value if you were having to use library
books or other borrowed material.

	Globalists	Traditionalists	Transformationalists
What is globalization?	Ch. 1, Sects 2.1-3.2 Ch. 1, pp. 22, 24-5 Ch. 3, Sect. 2.1, p. 90	Ch. 1, pp. 23-5 Ch. 3, Sect. 2.2, p. 91, Sect. 3	Ch. 1, pp. 23-4, 25 Ch. 3, Sect. 2.3, p. 91
How significant is contemporary globalization?	Ch. 2, Sect. 2 Ch. 3, Sects 1, 2.1	Ch. 2, Sect. 3 Ch. 3, Sects 2.2, 2.4, 4.1, 5	Ch. 2, Sect. 4
What is the impact of globalization on the sovereignty and autonomy of nation-states?	Ch. 4, Sects 2.2, 2.3, 3.2	Ch. 4, Sect. 3.1	Ch. 4, Sects 2.4, 3.3, 4, 5
Are there winners and losers in globalization?	Ch. 1, pp. 22-3 Ch. 2, Sects 2.2, 2.3 Ch. 4, p. 151	Ch. 3, pp. 110-13 Ch. 4, p. 151	Ch. 4, p. 151
Evidence for	Ch. 1, pp. 15-21 Ch. 1, Sect. 5 Ch. 2, pp. 49-54 Ch. 4, pp. 128-30, 135-48	Ch. 2, pp. 66-71 Ch. 3, Sects 4, 5 Ch. 4, p. 152	Ch. 2, pp. 72-5 Ch. 4, Sects 2.4, 3.3, 4, 5
Key evidence against	Ch. 3, Sect. 4.1 Ch. 4, Sect. 3.3	Ch. 1, pp. 15-21 Ch. 2, pp. 49-54 Ch. 4, Sect. 2.2	Ch. 2, Sects 2.3, 3.1, 3.2 Ch. 3, Sect. 4.1
Place of theory in wider political ideologies	Ch. 2, pp. 55-7, 63-5 Ch. 3, p. 89	Ch. 3, p. 89	

5.3 The course themes revisited

In the introduction to this workbook we noted that despite the change of focus from the United Kingdom to global issues, the issues raised by the course themes remain relevant.

- To what extent are we living in a more *diverse* and/or *uncertain* world?
- How much scope do individual *agents* have to determine their own destinies?
- How important are global *structures* in shaping local and national action?
- In terms of *knowledge and knowing*, how do we study social behaviour and structures and how valid is our evidence?

As we hope you have seen, the questions of a diverse and/or uncertain world are much of what the debates about globalization have been about. Some theorists supporting the globalist view have seen uniformity replacing diversity – global communications, technology, the ubiquitous McDonald's, the removal of barriers to trade, migration, etc. can all be cited. Transformationalists, in particular, argue that the uncertainties over what is taking place mean significant changes to our ways of life, social and economic structures, and the state, but that we don't fully understand or can predict the direction of change. Traditionalists provide a direct contrast to this, claiming that little of significance has changed.

Questions of studying society and the validity of evidence have also been at the forefront of what we have been studying. In particular we have looked at quantitative data as evidence and we have examined several forms of data presentation. More than anything else, however, this block of the course has been concerned with how to evaluate conflicting theories.

Perhaps the least up front of the course themes has been *structure and agency*, but debates about structure and agency have been important in informing many of the arguments.

WORKBOOK ACTIVITY 5.4

Look again through your notes on Chapter I and mark places where the theme of structure and agency has been relevant.

COMMENT _____

Our notes on this for Chapter 1 are:

AGENCY/STRUCTURE DEBATES

- Feelings of lack of control = poss. of structural changes beyond individual agency
- State structures unable to solve either big or small problems – cannot deliver to their peoples

- Dominance of markets by major players, eg Microsoft
- Creation of global pool of potentially powerless migrant labour
- Pollution caused by others, eg effects of Chernobyl
- Cochrane & Pain suggest globalization provides the structure in which individual agents can influence major institutions
- The super-rich have agency - they can escape into isolation

WORKBOOK ACTIVITY 5.5

Now have a go at filling in this grid.

Structure and agency in Block 4
Chapter 2
Chapter 3

	Structure and agency in Block 4
Chapter 4	
TV 04	

6 ASSESSING BLOCK 4

Your work on the critical evaluation of theories has been leading up to the assignment for this block of the course. In order to help you with this, we want to look at a particular question that is illustrative of the question you will actually be answering and make some comments on how to tackle it.

In approximately 1,500 words, discuss the view that the UK has lost its political and economic sovereignty in a global system.

Although this is not the actual TMA you are being asked to answer this year, as with the earlier specimen assignments, it is essentially the same type of question and will draw upon much of the same material. Therefore, working through the points below should be of direct benefit when you come to face the actual question.

At this point you may find it useful to quickly read through Sections 7.2–7.4 of *Workbook 2* where valuable general advice on essay writing was given and to consult the study skills index at the back of this workbook for other sources of advice.

When we look at an essay question we are being asked to answer, several key issues immediately come to mind:

- What type of question is it?

- What length of answer is required?

- What is the central subject matter?

- What terms need defining?

- What are the key arguments and conflicting theories on offer?

- Where will I locate my main sources of evidence?

- What will my basic conclusion be?

- How will I structure my answer?

By asking these at the very outset, we can save a great deal of time and effort in the long run. It means that any reading will be directed to those sections of immediate relevance to the task in hand, and any notes can be collected under the appropriate sub-headings.

Right – so looking at each of these issues we will offer answers for your consideration.

- **What type of question is it?** The key process word here is *discuss* (see the discussion of process words in *Workbook 1*, Section 7.2 and the Appendix in *Workbook 1*). As soon as we see *discuss* in any question we know there will be a debate in which there are several possible answers. Logically, a debate can only take place when there are at least two points of view. From this we know we are expected to show knowledge of those competing views, and there is a requirement to reach a clear conclusion. That does not mean we must totally identify with one view, although we might decide that is the appropriate outcome. It does mean that we should be clear as to our position on the strengths and weaknesses of each view.

- **What length of answer is required?** In this case the question expressly states that approximately 1,500 words are required. This indicates to us that the people who set the question believe that it cannot adequately be answered in a much shorter piece of work. Moreover, the skills that are being tested include careful choice of appropriate material and the succinct expression of analysis of it. Obviously we vary in our styles of writing and it would be wrong to expect us to express ourselves in precisely the same ways, so some flexibility of length is built in. We would generally expect a 10 per cent variation either way to be perfectly acceptable to the marker; and we would certainly expect to be penalized if this particular question were answered in more than 2,000 words.

- **What is the central subject matter?** The question is, in one sense, pretty specific. It indicates that the UK is the focus, so it would therefore be a mistake to bring in lots of material on any other states. It specifies the loss of political and economic sovereignty, suggesting that Chapters 3 and 4 are important, but it must be remembered that the two earlier chapters helped to set up the debates; certainly global culture and communications do have political and economic implications – so relevant points from Chapter 2 should be taken into account and the material on environmental issues in Chapter 1 might also be relevant.

- **What terms need defining?** The key term to deal with here is 'sovereignty', which concerns the moral and legal authority of a state to monopolize the making of laws and the use of force in a particular territory. The reference to 'economic' in addition to 'political' would suggest that some reference to regulations on trade, production, taxation policies, etc. would be particularly relevant, so an indication of this at the outset of the essay would be useful.

- **What are the key arguments and conflicting theories on offer?** Even if you had not studied the book, the very question would indicate that there are at least two possible views – yes, the UK has lost its sovereignty vs. no, it has not. Having read the material, however, you should be able to identify the contrasting views of the so-called globalists, traditionalists and transformationalists as constituting the conflicting theories on offer.

- **Where will I locate my main sources of evidence?** As indicated above, Chapters 3 and 4 are central to this question, but Chapters 1 and 2 also have relevance. Consider too if any of the TV and audio tapes etc. provide useful examples. Also, do not neglect what you have already studied in earlier books – the course themes of uncertainty and diversity, structure and agency, and knowledge and knowing link the material from across the course, so a reference to a course theme or to an example linked by it from another block may well be appropriate.

- **What will my basic conclusion be?** This is the key – at the beginning of this workbook we outlined some ways of evaluating theories. In this block you have been presented with three theories, and you need to apply those criteria to decide which theory is the most coherent, comprehensive, etc. As we said above, you do not need to argue that one is perfect and the others wrong, but you should have some clear idea of the strengths and weaknesses of each. In the social sciences there are always several possible answers, so it matters little which answer you plump for – it is the quality of your justification that matters.

- **How will I structure my answer?** This, to some extent, is a personal matter of style, so all we can offer you here is our approach. We would:

  (a) Begin with a short introduction which would map out our intentions – to outline the evidence of loss of sovereignty, describe and examine the three contrasting theories, and to conclude that although it has some deficiencies, theory *x* seems to be the soundest.

  (b) Outline the evidence of globalization for the UK – global trade patterns, the international media, cultural influences, the drug trade, international organizations, etc.

  (c) Describe in turn each of the three theories, indicating possible strengths and weaknesses.

  (d) Conclude with reasons why the statement is generally true or untrue.

  These points can be represented in the form of a diagram:

INTRODUCTION	EVIDENCE	DISCUSSION	CONCLUSION
• definition • outline of intent	• trade patterns • global media Disney/McDonald's • global crime organizations	• outline of Theory 1 • comment on strengths/weaknesses • ditto Theory 2 • ditto Theory 3	• indicate weakness of preferred theory • stress relative strength of this theory over others

Remember to keep using key words from the question in critical places – for example, the opening sentences of paragraphs – to ensure you are answering the question as set (see especially *Workbook 2*, Section 7.4.3).

Now turn to the *Assignments Booklet* for TMA 04.

Best of luck!

REFERENCE

Lukes, S. (1981) 'Fact and theory in the social sciences' in Potter, D. *et al.* (eds) *Society and the Social Sciences: An Introduction*, London, Routledge and Kegan Paul.

ACKNOWLEDGEMENTS

Cover

Image copyright © 1996 PhotoDisc, Inc.

We would like to thank Robert Kelly (jnr) for his help with sections on quantitative data.

STUDY SKILLS INDEX

IWB = *Introductory Workbook*
WB1 = *Workbook 1*
WB2 = *Workbook 2*
WB3 = *Workbook 3*
MCR = *Mid Course Review*
WB4 = *Workbook 4*
AC7A = *Notes for Audio-cassette 7* (Side A)